~A BINGO BOOK~

Indiana
Bingo Book

COMPLETE BINGO GAME IN A BOOK

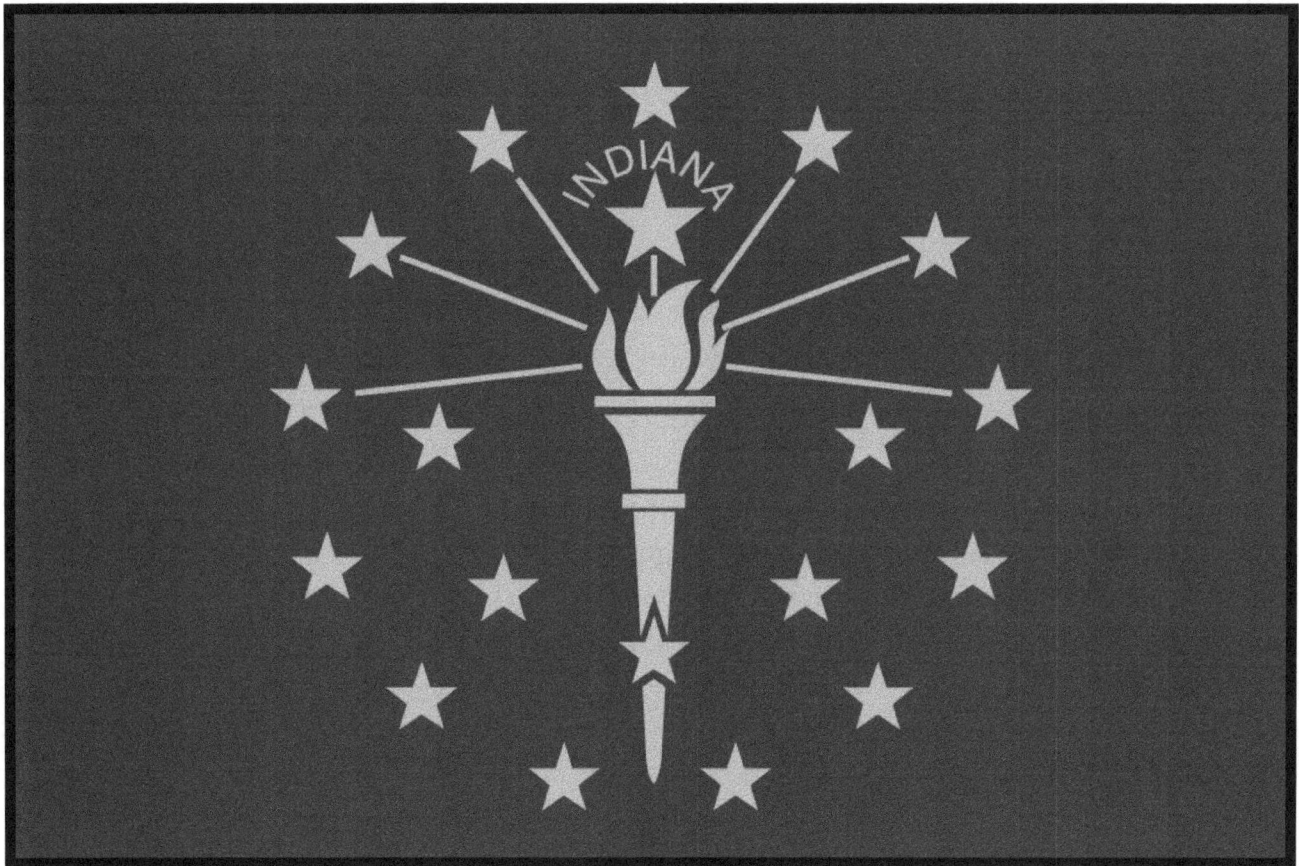

Written By Rebecca Stark

ISBN 978-0-87386-507-4

Educational Books 'n' Bingo

Printed in the U.S.A.

DIRECTIONS

INCLUDED:

> List of Terms
>
> Templates for Additional Terms and Clues
>
> 2 Clues per Term
>
> 30 Unique Bingo Sheets (To cut out or copy)
>
> Sheet of Markers (to copy and distribute)

1. **Either cut apart the book or make copies of ALL the sheets. You might want to make an extra copy of the clue sheets to use for introduction and review. Keep the sheets in an envelope for easy reuse.**

2. Cut apart the call sheets with terms and clues.

3. Pass out one bingo sheet per student. There are enough unique sheets for a class of 30.

4. Pass out the markers. You may cut apart the markers included in this book or use any other small items of your choice. Students can also mark the sheets themselves; recopy the sheets as needed for additional games.

5. Decide whether or not you will require the entire sheet to be filled. Requiring the entire sheet to be filled provides a better review. However, if you have a short time to fill, you may prefer to have them do the just the border or some other format. Tell the class before you begin what is required.

6. There are 50 terms. Read the list before you begin. If there are any terms that have not been covered in class, you may want to read to the students the term and clues before you begin.

7. There is a blank space in the middle of each sheet. You can instruct the students to use it as a free space or you can write in answers to cover terms not included. Of course, in this case you would create your own clues. (Templates provided.)

8. Shuffle the sheets and place them in a pile. Two or three clues are provided for each term. If you plan to play the game with the same group more than once, you might want to choose a different clue for each game. If not, you may choose to use more than one clue.

9. Be sure to keep the sheets you have used for the present game in a separate pile. When a student calls, "Bingo," he or she will have to verify that the correct answers are on his or her sheet AND that the markers were placed in response to the proper questions. Pull out the sheets that are on the student's sheet keeping them in the order they were used in the game. Read each clue as it was given and ask the student to identify the correct answer from his or her sheet.

10. If the student has the correct answers on the sheet AND has shown that they were marked in response to the *correct questions,* then that student is the winner and the game is over. If the student does not have the correct answers on the sheet OR he or she marked the answers in response to *the wrong questions,* then the game continues until there is a proper winner.

11. If you want to play again, reshuffle the sheets and begin again.

Have fun

TERMS INCLUDED

Agricultural	Legislative Branch
Angel Mounds	Limberlost Swamp
Border(s)	Limestone
Cardinal	Lincoln
Central Indiana	Michiana
Chicago Metropolitan Area	Motor Speedway
Civil War	Motto
Climate	Northern Indiana
Corydon	Ohio River
County (-ies)	Old Richmond
Eiteljorg Museum	Peony
Evansville	Regions
Executive Branch	Seal
Flag	South Bend
Fort Ouiatenon	Southern Plains and Lowlands
Fort Wayne	Theodore Clement Steele
Benjamin Harrison	Tecumseh
William Henry Harrison	Till Plains
Hoosier(s)	Time Zone
Indiana Day	Tulip
Indiana Dunes	Underground Railroad
Indianapolis	University
Industry (-ies)	Vincennes
Judicial Branch	Wabash
Lake Michigan	Wilbur Wright

Additional Terms

Choose as many additional terms as you would like and write them in the
squares. Repeat each as desired.
Cut out the squares and randomly distribute them to the class.
Instruct the students to place their square on the center space of their card.

Indiana Bingo

© Barbara M. Peller

Clues for Additional Terms

Write three clues for each of your additional terms.

<table>
<tr><td>

1. _____

2.

3.

</td><td>

1. _____

2.

3.

</td></tr>
<tr><td>

1. _____

2.

3.

</td><td>

1. _____

2.

3.

</td></tr>
<tr><td>

1. _____

2.

3.

</td><td>

1. _____

2.

3.

</td></tr>
</table>

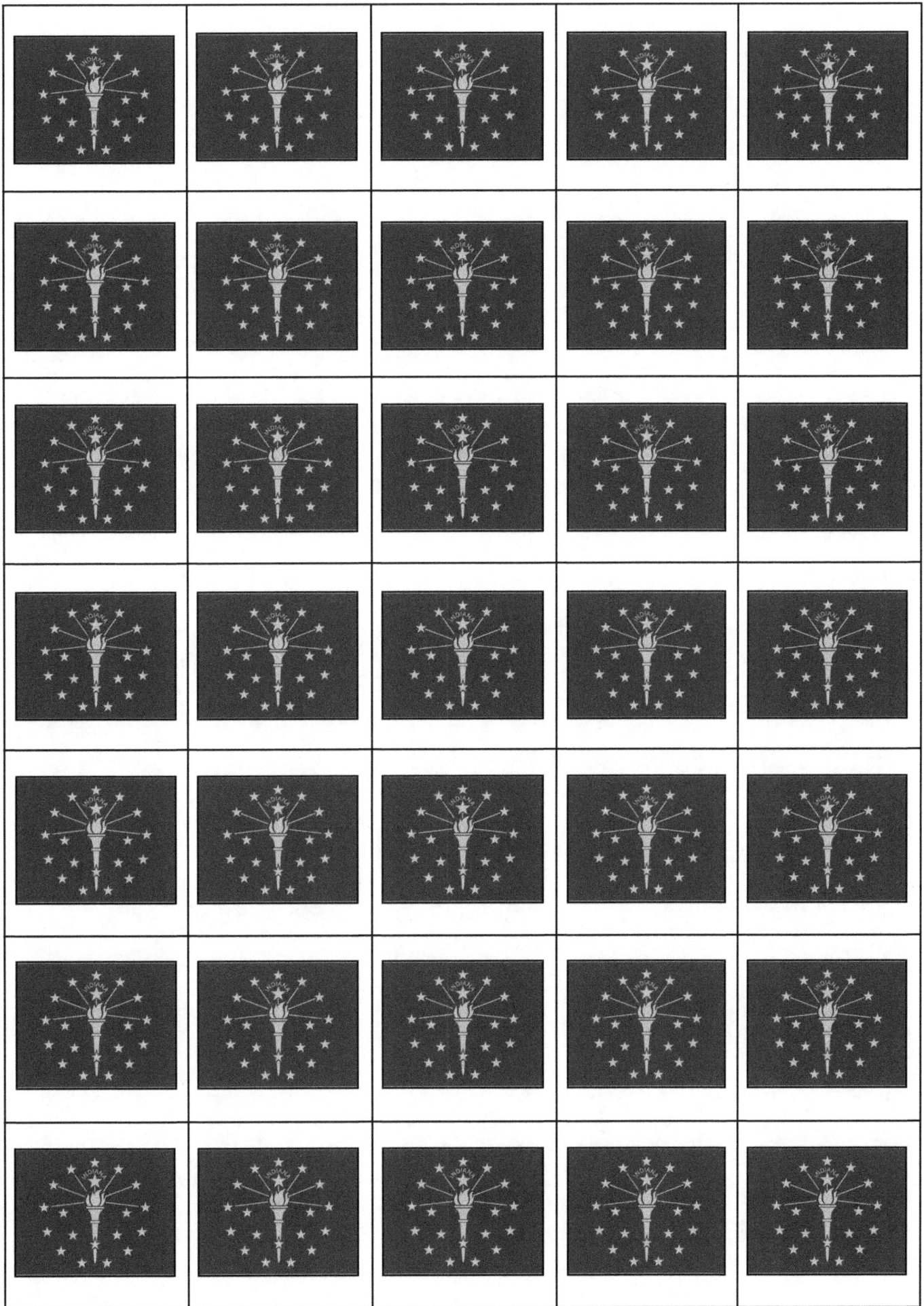

Agricultural 1. Corn, hogs, soybeans, wheat, oats, rye, tomatoes, onions, and poultry are important ___ products. 2. Corn is the most important ___ product.	**Angel Mounds** 1. ___ is one of the best preserved prehistoric Native American sites in the United States. 2. ___ was once occupied by Native Americans whom archaeologists call Mississippians.
Border(s) 1. Illinois, Kentucky, Michigan, and Ohio ___ Indiana. 2. Lake Michigan and the Ohio River are both water ___ of the state.	**Cardinal** 1. The northern ___ is the state bird of Indiana. 2. The male ___ is a vibrant red, while the female is a dull red-brown shade.
Central Indiana 1. Indianapolis is in ___, which comprises 33 counties. A large part of ___ is referred to as the Indianapolis Metropolitan Area. 2. Cities in this part of the state include ties include Indianapolis, Lafayette, Anderson, Muncie, and Terre Haute.	**Chicago Metropolitan Area** 1. The northwestern part of Indiana is often thought of as the ___. 2. Gary, Indiana, is considered part of the ___.
Civil War 1. The Battle of Corydon was the only ___ battle that took place in Indiana. 2. Indiana fought on the Union side during the ___.	**Climate** 1. Most of Indiana has a humid continental ___ with cool winters and warm, wet summers. 2. The extreme southern part of the state has a humid subtropical ___ .
Corydon 1. ___ was the second capital of the and the first Indiana state capital. 2. In 1825 the state capital was moved from ___ to Indianapolis because the population center of Indiana had shifted northward.	**County (-ies)** 1. The are 92 ___ in Indiana. 2. There are 26 ___ in the Northern Indiana, 33 in Central Indiana, and 33 in Southern Indiana.

Indiana Bingo

Eiteljorg Museum 1. The ___ features American Indian and Western Art. 2. The ___ is part of Indianapolis's White River State Park.	**Evansville** 1. ___ is the third largest city in Indiana after Indianapolis and Fort Wayne. 2. This city in the southwestern part of the state is situated on the Ohio River.
Executive Branch 1. The governor is the head of the ___. The present-day governor is [fill in]. 2. The governor, lieutenant governor, and attorney general, auditor, and treasurer are part of the ___.	**Flag** 1. The state ___ depicts a gold torch on a field of blue. The torch represents liberty and enlightenment. 2. There are 19 stars on the state___, one for each state at the time of Indiana's admission to the Union. The largest star right above the torch represents Indiana.
Fort Ouiatenon 1. This French settlement was the first fortified European settlement in what is now Indiana. 2. ___ was established by the French in 1717 to prevent British expansion into the Ohio and Wabash country.	**Fort Wayne** 1. This city in the northeastern part of the state is the second largest city in Indiana. 2. ___ was established at the confluence of the St. Joseph River, St. Marys River, and Maumee River.
Benjamin Harrison 1. ___ was the 23rd President of the United States. 2. ___'s grandfather was President William Henry Harrison.	**William Henry Harrison** 1. ___ gained fame for leading U.S. forces against Native Americans at the Battle of Tippecanoe in 1811. He based his campaign slogan, "Tippecanoe and Tyler, Too," on this success. 2. ___ was the first governor of and the 9th President of the United States.
Hoosier(s) 1. People from Indiana are called ___. 2. Indiana is called the ___ State. Indiana Bingo	**Indiana Day** 1. ___ is observed every December 11. 2. ___ marks the anniversary of the admission of Indiana to the Union. © Barbara M. Peller

Indiana Dunes 1. The ___ National Lakeshore is in northwest Indiana and is managed by the National Park Service. 2. The ___ National Lakeshore runs for almost 25 miles along the southern shore of Lake Michigan.	**Indianapolis** 1. ___ is the capital of Indiana. It is the largest city in Indiana and the second largest of all the state capitals. 2. Indiana War Memorial Plaza Historic District, which includes the Soldiers and Sailors Monument, is in this capital city___.
Industry (-ies) 1. The manufacture of steel, electric equipment, transportation equipment, and machinery are important ___. 2. Mining of bituminous coal is an important ___.	**Judicial Branch** 1. The ___ interprets what our laws mean and makes decisions about the laws and those who break them. 2. It is made up of several courts, the highest of which is the state Supreme Court.
Lake Michigan 1. Indiana has over 40 miles of shoreline on ___. 2. The Indiana Dunes National Lakeshore runs along the southern shore of ___.	**Legislative Branch** 1. The General Assembly is the ___ of government; it comprises the Senate and the House of Representatives. 2. The ___ makes the laws.
Limberlost Swamp 1. At the turn of the century, the ___ was described as a "treacherous swamp and quagmire." 2. The ___ was known for its quicksand and unsavory characters. It got its name from the fate of Jim Corbus, known as "Limber Jim." He went hunting and never returned.	**Limestone** 1. Indiana has one of the largest ___ quarry regions in the United States. 2. Thirty-five of the 50 state capitol buildings were made of Indiana limestone.
Lincoln 1. President ___ spent his boyhood—from 1816 to 1830—in southern Indiana. His home was in what was Perry County then, but Spencer County today. 2. The ___ Boyhood National Memorial was the first national park established in Indiana.	**Michiana** 1. ___ is a region in northern Indiana and southwestern Michigan. 2. ___ centers on the city of South Bend, Indiana.

Motor Speedway	**Motto**
1. Automobile races are held at the Indianapolis ___. 2. The ___ was established in 1909. The year 2011 marked the 100th anniversary of the 500-Mile Race held here.	1. "The Crossroads of America" is the official state ___. 2. The state ___, "The Crossroads of America," began as a nickname for Indianapolis, which is the hub for several major Interstate highways.
Northern Indiana	**Ohio River**
1. Northern Indiana comprises 27 counties and includes Gary. 2. Much of this region is farmland; however, it also includes the Rust Belt in the eastern part of the region.	1. The ___ separates Indiana and Kentucky. 2. By volume, the ___ is the largest tributary of the Mississippi River.
Old Richmond	**Peony**
1. This historic district in Wayne County was first settled by members of the Society of Friends; it was later settled by free blacks and German immigrants. 2. This historic district is sometimes called "German Village."	1. The Indiana state flower is the ___. 2. The ___ was adopted as the state flower in 1957. From 1931 to 1957 the zinnia was the state flower.
Regions	**Seal**
1. There are 3 main geographic ___ regions. 2. The 3 main geographic ___ of Indiana are The Great Lakes Plain in the north, the Till Plains in the center, and the Southern Plains and Lowlands in the south.	1. A buffalo, a woodsman, sycamore trees, hills and a setting sun are symbols on the Great ___ of Indiana. 2. Leaves of the state tree, the tulip tree, are on the border of the Great ___.
South Bend	**Southern Plains and Lowlands**
1. ___ is the cultural and economic center of the Michiana region. 2. ___ is on the southernmost bend of the St. Joseph River.	1. The ___ region is characterized by a series of "knobs," or steep hills, divided by lowlands. 2. Several caverns, including Marengo and Wyandotte caves, have been carved in the limestone by underground streams in the ___ region.

Indiana Bingo

Theodore Clement Steele 1. This Impressionist painter was known for his Indiana landscapes. 2. ___ was one of the "Hoosier Group" of American Impressionist painters.	**Tecumseh** 1. ___, a Shawnee chief, tried to assemble a confederation of tribes to resist white settlement. 2. This Shawnee leader allied himself with British forces during the War of 1812.
Till Plains 1. The ___ are south of the Great Lake Plains. They are part of the Corn Belt. 2. The landscape of the ___ consists of gently rolling hills and valleys. Hoosier Hill, the highest point in the state at 1,257 feet above sea level, is in this region.	**Time Zone** 1. Most of Indiana is in the Eastern ___. 2. A small portion of western Indiana in the Central ___.
Tulip 1. The ___ tree is the official state tree. 2. The ___ tree is a valuable timber and shade tree. It is fast growing and the tallest of the eastern hardwoods.	**Underground Railroad** 1. The ___ was a network of secret routes and safe houses used by 19th-century slaves to escape to free states and Canada. 2. Levi Coffin's home is sometimes called the "Grand Central Station of the ___."
University 1. Bloomington and Indianapolis are the main campuses of Indiana ___. 2. West Lafayette is the main campus of Purdue ___.	**Vincennes** 1. This city on the Wabash River was founded by French traders in 1732. It is the oldest continually inhabited European settlement in Indiana. 2. Indiana Territory was formed from the Northwest Territory. ___ was its first capital.
Wabash 1. The ___ River is the longest free-flowing river east of the Mississippi. 2. The White River is a tributary of the ___ River.	**Wilbur Wright** 1. This inventor and aviation pioneer was born near Millville, Indiana, in 1867. 2. He and his brother are credited with inventing and building the world's first successful airplane.

Indiana Bingo

Seal	Agricultural	William Henry Harrison	Hoosier(s)	Cardinal
Fort Wayne	Angel Mounds	Vincennes	Michiana	Theodore Clement Steele
University	Lincoln		Old Richmond	Wabash
Underground Railroad	Southern Plains and Lowlands	Tulip	Limestone	Motto
Ohio River	Indianapolis	Executive Branch	Time Zone	Lake Michigan

Indiana Bingo

Underground Railroad	University	Judicial Branch	South Bend	Limberlost Swamp
Motto	Flag	Civil War	Southern Plains and Lowlands	Northern Indiana
Corydon	Indianapolis		Industry (-ies)	Tulip
Peony	Regions	Lincoln	Wilbur Wright	Cardinal
Theodore Clement Steele	Vincennes	Executive Branch	Fort Wayne	Time Zone

© Barbara M. Peller

Indiana Bingo

Indianapolis	Tulip	Flag	Limestone	University
Motto	Angel Mounds	Climate	Agricultural	Indiana Day
Southern Plains and Lowlands	Vincennes		Northern Indiana	Border(s)
Lincoln	Corydon	Ohio River	Peony	Judicial Branch
Time Zone	County (-ies)	Executive Branch	Wilbur Wright	Limberlost Swamp

Indiana Bingo: Card No. 3

Indiana Bingo

Lincoln	Northern Indiana	William Henry Harrison	County (-ies)	Limberlost Swamp
Motor Speedway	Chicago Metropolitan Area	Agricultural	South Bend	University
Old Richmond	Peony		Lake Michigan	Hoosier(s)
Tulip	Angel Mounds	Vincennes	Executive Branch	Civil War
Eiteljorg Museum	Theodore Clement Steele	Central Indiana	Time Zone	Wabash

Indiana Bingo

Theodore Clement Steele	Cardinal	Southern Plains and Lowlands	Civil War	County (-ies)
Motor Speedway	Tulip	Climate	Industry (-ies)	Angel Mounds
William Henry Harrison	Wabash		Michiana	Indiana Dunes
Lake Michigan	Limberlost Swamp	Seal	Wilbur Wright	Evansville
Flag	Executive Branch	University	Lincoln	Old Richmond

Indiana Bingo

Border(s)	Northern Indiana	Judicial Branch	Limberlost Swamp	Wabash
Limestone	Southern Plains and Lowlands	Evansville	Agricultural	University
South Bend	Eiteljorg Museum		Chicago Metropolitan Area	Industry (-ies)
Executive Branch	Ohio River	Wilbur Wright	Central Indiana	William Henry Harrison
Motto	Civil War	Seal	Old Richmond	Fort Ouiatenon

Indiana Bingo

Seal	Northern Indiana	Indiana Dunes	Tulip	Flag
Motto	Limberlost Swamp	Indianapolis	Angel Mounds	Motor Speedway
Wabash	Hoosier(s)		Industry (-ies)	Chicago Metropolitan Area
Lincoln	Peony	Climate	Underground Railroad	Corydon
Executive Branch	County (-ies)	Wilbur Wright	Central Indiana	Border(s)

Indiana Bingo

Old Richmond	Northern Indiana	Benjamin Harrison	Limestone	Chicago Metropolitan Area
Motor Speedway	William Henry Harrison	South Bend	Wabash	Civil War
Fort Ouiatenon	County (-ies)		Limberlost Swamp	Cardinal
Time Zone	Lincoln	Underground Railroad	Eiteljorg Museum	Peony
Vincennes	Executive Branch	Central Indiana	Southern Plains and Lowlands	Motto

Indiana Bingo

Industry (-ies)	Flag	Indianapolis	Fort Ouiatenon	County (-ies)
Eiteljorg Museum	Limberlost Swamp	Old Richmond	Southern Plains and Lowlands	Northern Indiana
Indiana Day	Seal		Angel Mounds	Benjamin Harrison
Evansville	Cardinal	Ohio River	Michiana	Indiana Dunes
Peony	Wilbur Wright	Climate	Underground Railroad	Lake Michigan

Indiana Bingo

Underground Railroad	Limestone	Chicago Metropolitan Area	South Bend	Fort Ouiatenon
Wabash	Civil War	Agricultural	Angel Mounds	Limberlost Swamp
County (-ies)	Northern Indiana		Hoosier(s)	Corydon
Ohio River	Lake Michigan	Evansville	Wilbur Wright	Indiana Day
Climate	Motto	Judicial Branch	Theodore Clement Steele	Old Richmond

Indiana Bingo

Border(s)	Northern Indiana	Southern Plains and Lowlands	Evansville	Motto
Benjamin Harrison	Indiana Day	Michiana	Industry (-ies)	Agricultural
Motor Speedway	Limberlost Swamp		Judicial Branch	Indianapolis
Climate	University	Wilbur Wright	County (-ies)	Underground Railroad
Eiteljorg Museum	Executive Branch	Seal	Central Indiana	Flag

Indiana Bingo

Flag	Cardinal	Indiana Day	Limestone	Industry (-ies)
Indianapolis	Motto	William Henry Harrison	Central Indiana	Angel Mounds
Seal	Indiana Dunes		Wabash	South Bend
Executive Branch	Peony	Limberlost Swamp	Underground Railroad	Motor Speedway
Northern Indiana	Benjamin Harrison	County (-ies)	Eiteljorg Museum	Civil War

Indiana Bingo

Evansville	Cardinal	Border(s)	Indiana Day	Wabash
William Henry Harrison	Benjamin Harrison	Limberlost Swamp	Industry (-ies)	Corydon
Limestone	Civil War		Indianapolis	Indiana Dunes
Old Richmond	Wilbur Wright	Chicago Metropolitan Area	County (-ies)	Underground Railroad
Executive Branch	Lake Michigan	Central Indiana	Seal	Michiana

Indiana Bingo

Fort Wayne	Limberlost Swamp	Southern Plains and Lowlands	Industry (-ies)	Eiteljorg Museum
Civil War	Seal	Indiana Day	Angel Mounds	Northern Indiana
Evansville	Hoosier(s)		Judicial Branch	Climate
Lake Michigan	Wilbur Wright	County (-ies)	Chicago Metropolitan Area	Border(s)
Executive Branch	South Bend	Corydon	Motto	Old Richmond

Indiana Bingo

Michiana	Industry (-ies)	Southern Plains and Lowlands	Flag	Limestone
Border(s)	Judicial Branch	Agricultural	William Henry Harrison	Eiteljorg Museum
Wabash	Seal		University	Northern Indiana
Executive Branch	Indiana Day	Benjamin Harrison	Wilbur Wright	Evansville
Motto	Peony	Central Indiana	Fort Ouiatenon	Indianapolis

Indiana Bingo

Chicago Metropolitan Area	Indiana Day	Benjamin Harrison	Fort Ouiatenon	Regions
South Bend	Corydon	Indiana Dunes	Motor Speedway	Hoosier(s)
Evansville	Cardinal		Wabash	Indianapolis
Lincoln	Civil War	Executive Branch	Michiana	Underground Railroad
Eiteljorg Museum	Till Plains	Central Indiana	Peony	Northern Indiana

Indiana Bingo: Card No. 16

Indiana Bingo

Climate	Tecumseh	Legislative Branch	Indiana Day	Fort Wayne
Michiana	Eiteljorg Museum	Wilbur Wright	Hoosier(s)	Indiana Dunes
Industry (-ies)	Old Richmond		Till Plains	Benjamin Harrison
Lake Michigan	Motto	Underground Railroad	Southern Plains and Lowlands	Corydon
Ohio River	Evansville	Flag	Limestone	Cardinal

Indiana Bingo: Card No. 17

Indiana
Bingo

Fort Ouiatenon	County (-ies)	Civil War	Evansville	South Bend
Northern Indiana	Climate	Ohio River	Wabash	Eiteljorg Museum
Industry (-ies)	Corydon		Legislative Branch	William Henry Harrison
Cardinal	Agricultural	Wilbur Wright	Underground Railroad	Judicial Branch
Till Plains	Indiana Day	Southern Plains and Lowlands	Tecumseh	Border(s)

Indiana Bingo: Card No. 18

Indiana Bingo

Wabash	Border(s)	Indiana Day	Benjamin Harrison	Underground Railroad
Michiana	Limestone	Northern Indiana	Flag	Hoosier(s)
Tecumseh	County (-ies)		Angel Mounds	University
Judicial Branch	Till Plains	Ohio River	Peony	Legislative Branch
William Henry Harrison	Regions	Motto	Old Richmond	Central Indiana

Indiana Bingo: Card No. 19

© Barbara M. Peller

Indiana Bingo

Fort Wayne	Tecumseh	Limestone	Indiana Day	Central Indiana
Civil War	Indianapolis	Motor Speedway	Ohio River	South Bend
Cardinal	Indiana Dunes		Lincoln	Agricultural
Theodore Clement Steele	Vincennes	Time Zone	Peony	Till Plains
Tulip	Old Richmond	Regions	Underground Railroad	Legislative Branch

Indiana Bingo

Michiana	Border(s)	Motor Speedway	Indiana Day	Theodore Clement Steele
Cardinal	Legislative Branch	Chicago Metropolitan Area	Benjamin Harrison	Seal
Corydon	Motto		Tecumseh	Southern Plains and Lowlands
Ohio River	Flag	Till Plains	Lake Michigan	Old Richmond
Lincoln	Regions	Central Indiana	Climate	Peony

Indiana Bingo

Fort Ouiatenon	Judicial Branch	Legislative Branch	William Henry Harrison	Evansville
South Bend	Limestone	University	Benjamin Harrison	Angel Mounds
Civil War	Hoosier(s)		Seal	Indiana Dunes
Till Plains	Lake Michigan	Peony	Agricultural	Motor Speedway
Regions	Climate	Tecumseh	Corydon	Lincoln

Indiana Bingo

Chicago Metropolitan Area	Tecumseh	Flag	William Henry Harrison	Central Indiana
Border(s)	Fort Wayne	Motto	Michiana	Agricultural
Judicial Branch	Evansville		Time Zone	Seal
Corydon	Regions	Till Plains	Climate	Peony
Theodore Clement Steele	Vincennes	Old Richmond	Ohio River	Legislative Branch

Indiana Bingo

Chicago Metropolitan Area	Old Richmond	Fort Wayne	Tecumseh	Benjamin Harrison
Legislative Branch	Central Indiana	Motor Speedway	South Bend	Seal
Indiana Dunes	Fort Ouiatenon		Evansville	Corydon
Theodore Clement Steele	Time Zone	Till Plains	Climate	Cardinal
Tulip	Lincoln	Regions	Limestone	Vincennes

Indiana Bingo

Lincoln	Motor Speedway	Tecumseh	Southern Plains and Lowlands	Legislative Branch
Agricultural	Cardinal	Michiana	Chicago Metropolitan Area	Angel Mounds
Lake Michigan	Benjamin Harrison		Time Zone	Till Plains
University	Theodore Clement Steele	Vincennes	Regions	Hoosier(s)
Central Indiana	Fort Wayne	Civil War	Eiteljorg Museum	Tulip

Indiana Bingo: Card No. 25

Indiana Bingo

Legislative Branch	Tecumseh	Judicial Branch	South Bend	Fort Ouiatenon
Ohio River	Limestone	Benjamin Harrison	Fort Wayne	Chicago Metropolitan Area
Lake Michigan	Time Zone		Hoosier(s)	Lincoln
Climate	William Henry Harrison	Theodore Clement Steele	Regions	Till Plains
Indiana Dunes	Eiteljorg Museum	Southern Plains and Lowlands	Vincennes	Tulip

Indiana Bingo

Judicial Branch	Civil War	Tecumseh	Fort Wayne	Indianapolis
Theodore Clement Steele	Time Zone	Michiana	Till Plains	Angel Mounds
Wilbur Wright	Vincennes		Regions	Lincoln
Fort Ouiatenon	Border(s)	Motor Speedway	Tulip	Agricultural
Eiteljorg Museum	Hoosier(s)	Legislative Branch	University	Indiana Dunes

Indiana Bingo

Judicial Branch	Fort Wayne	University	Tecumseh	Chicago Metropolitan Area
Indianapolis	Legislative Branch	Time Zone	South Bend	Hoosier(s)
Vincennes	Corydon		Indiana Dunes	Ohio River
Underground Railroad	Fort Ouiatenon	Motto	Regions	Till Plains
William Henry Harrison	Industry (-ies)	Eiteljorg Museum	Tulip	Theodore Clement Steele

Indiana Bingo

Legislative Branch	Fort Wayne	Fort Ouiatenon	Michiana	Industry (-ies)
Peony	Ohio River	Motor Speedway	Indiana Dunes	University
Lake Michigan	Time Zone		Angel Mounds	Tecumseh
Indianapolis	Theodore Clement Steele	Limberlost Swamp	Regions	Till Plains
Chicago Metropolitan Area	Benjamin Harrison	Tulip	Border(s)	Vincennes

Indiana
Bingo

County (-ies)	Tecumseh	South Bend	Industry (-ies)	Till Plains
Agricultural	Fort Wayne	Judicial Branch	Hoosier(s)	Angel Mounds
Lake Michigan	Evansville		Indiana Dunes	Motor Speedway
Tulip	Border(s)	William Henry Harrison	Regions	Time Zone
Theodore Clement Steele	Wabash	Vincennes	Legislative Branch	University

www.ingramcontent.com/pod-product-compliance
Lightning Source LLC
LaVergne TN
LVHW061337060426

835511LV00014B/1979